LONG LIVE THE KING!

When T'Challa returns home to the hidden, technologically advanced African nation of Wakanda to serve as his country's new leader, he is soon challenged for the throne from factions within his own country.

As two foes plot to destroy Wakanda, T'Challa, otherwise known as Black Panther, must team up with C.I.A. agent Everett K. Ross and members of the Dora Milaje, Wakandan special forces, to prevent Wakanda from being dragged into a world war.

TITAN EDITORIAL
Editor Jonathan Wilkins
Senior Editor Martin Eden
Editorial Assistants Tolly Maggs & Jake Devine
Art Director Oz Browne
Senior Production Controller Jackie Flook
Production Supervisor Maria Pearson
Production Controller Peter James
Senior Sales Manager Steve Tothill
Subscriptions Executive Tony Ho

Direct Sales & Marketing Manager Ricky Claydon
Advertising Assistant Tom Miller
Commercial Manager Michelle Fairlamb
Brand Manager, Marketing Lucy Ripper
U.S. Advertising Manager Jeni Smith
Publishing Manager Darryl Tothill
Publishing Director Chris Teather
Operations Director Leigh Baulch
Executive Director Vivian Cheung
Publisher Nick Landau

DISTRIBUTION
US Newsstand: Total Publisher Services, Inc.
John Dziewiatkowski, 630-851-7683
US Distribution: Curtis Circulation Company, I
ngram Periodicals
US Direct Sales Market: Diamond
Comic Distributors
For more info on advertising contact
adinfo@titanemail.com

Marvel Studios' *Black Panther* published by Titan Magazines, a
division of Titan Publishing Group
Limited, 144 Southwark Street, London SE1 0UP
For sale in the U.S. and Canada.

Printed in the US by Quad.
ISBN: 9781785866371

Contributors Nick Jones, David Manley-Leach
Thank you to Shiho Tilley, Beatrice Osman, and Eugene
Paraszczuk at Disney for all their help.

Titan Authorized User. No part of this publication may be
reproduced, stored in a retrieval system, or transmitted, in any
form or by any means, without the prior written permission of the
publisher. A CIP catalogue record for this title is available from
the British Library.

10 9 8 7 6 5 4 3 2 1

marvel.com
© 2018 MARVEL

CONTENTS

CHADWICK BOSEMAN IS
BLACK PANTHER

Following his show-stopping appearance in *Captain America: Civil War*, acclaimed actor Chadwick Boseman returns to the role of T'Challa, otherwise known as Black Panther.

Black Panther Movie Special: What was your exposure to Marvel prior to working on the films?
Chadwick Boseman: I'm a fan. I'd seen the *Iron Man* movies, the *Captain America* movies, and *The Avengers*. I'm not the type of guy that really collects comic books, but I knew all about the Black Panther character from reading them – particularly the Reginald Hudlin strips.

What was it about the character that appealed to you?
He's a Super Hero who is also a king. There's a James Bond feel to the character. He has a large amount of responsibility.

There's a lot of real world conflict that you can bring to the role, so you don't feel like you're just playing a guy in a suit. He's a conflicted, well-rounded character. If you're gonna play a Super Hero you want to do one where you can really act, where you can really do something that's going to make you a better artist as well.

And there's not a lot of opportunities to play an African Super Hero. It was just something that was breaking new ground.

What's it like being fully immersed in the Marvel Cinematic Universe?
There's a lot of excitement about the opportunity to make a standalone movie based upon the way the character was set up in *Captain America: Civil War*. I feel like that was a success that left people wanting more.

There was the opportunity in this film to really flesh out the Black Panther character, because in his last appearance I was a supporting character. In this movie, we had different aspects of the character that we wanted to show.

What was your reaction to the script?
I was happy that it was right on track from the beginning. You never know what the first draft is going to be like, but it was a pretty good one. The point of view of every character is well-thought out. It's not just explosions, fight scenes, and people flying around – it's a character piece, too.

Where do we find Black Panther as the story starts?
In *Civil War* he lost his father. He's discovering what that means for him. In *Civil War* he was trying to avenge his father's death. As *Black Panther* begins, T'Challa deals with his loss and faces the responsibility of becoming the new king. It's a great starting point because it gives T'Challa something to grapple with. ▶

▶ **Is this your first time working with the film's writer/director, Ryan Coogler?**
Yes. He has been very open and collaborative and he listens. I came in and did table-reads with some of the actors. He just did it like he was directing the scene. So I actually first worked with him on that part of the process.

How did you feel about the table-read process?
I like the process – not just on this film, but even on plays that I've done in the past. The table-read is always a good place for people to come into the process from wherever they want to. You can do it very objectively, or you can do it with a really strong point of view. You can do it in accent or out of accent – you can do it however you feel. You get a chance to get introduced to everybody's process of how they want to work. So I like that process in terms of learning about the other actors, and it provides an opportunity to see if things work or not.

"He's a Super Hero who is also a king. There's a James Bond feel to the character."

Are there differences to the Black Panther suit since we last saw it in *Captain America: Civil War*?
Yeah! There are some upgrades to the suit, thanks to T'Challa's sister!

What has stunt training been like?
It's cool! It's obviously intense, and a lot of work and sweat. I enjoyed working with the stunt team, JoJo Lambert and Clayton J.

01 Black Panther has a deadly confrontation with Erik Killmonger

02 Black Panther prepares to jump into battle

03 Chadwick Boseman takes command as T'Challa

04 Boseman as T'Challa heads out of his Royal Talon fighter with Nakia (Lupita Nyong'o) and Okoye (Danai Gurira)

06

BLACK PANTHER – A BRIEF COMIC BOOK HISTORY

Black Panther/ T'Challa was created by Stan Lee and Jack Kirby and first appeared in *Fantastic Four* #52 in 1966. The character is the king and protector of Wakanda, a fictional African nation. Black Panther is a talented scientist and strategist and a master of armed and unarmed combat. Black Panther's senses, strength, speed, and durability are enhanced to superhuman levels by his heart-shaped herb. He wears a vibranium suit and uses vibranium equipment. He has been a member of the Fantastic Four, the Avengers, and the Illuminati.

Barber, on the style of movement. That's one of the most fun things. It's like dancing. I wanted to make sure that there is some legitimate African movement and African martial arts shown in the film to tell the story of Wakanda as a military nation. Sometimes it feels like we're training for a real fight, you know?

What will audiences get out of *Black Panther*?
If it's just a normal movie or if it's just what audiences expect,

"I wanted some legitimate African martial arts in the film."

then that's not quite good enough. It has to be "Wow!" for many different reasons – in the performances, the spectacle, and the fight scenes.

How does Black Panther differ from the other Marvel Studios Super Heroes?

He looks good, he smells good, he feels good! I'm just kidding. He's a strategist and a world leader. That's a responsibility that other Super Heroes don't have. He has to look out for an entire nation and then also consider that nation's place in the world and how it affects the rest of the world. ■

05 Chadwick Boseman suited up as the heroic Black Panther

06 T'Challa gets ready to fight!

CONCEPT ART
T'Challa's vision, where he comes face to face with his alter ego's namesake.
Art by Vance Kovaks

MICHAEL B. JORDAN IS

ERIK KILLMONGER

Michael B. Jordan's acting résumé has been growing and becoming ever more amazing over the last few years – and he's hit the jackpot again by playing a Marvel supervillain in *Black Panther*. Here, Jordan discusses his role as Erik Killmonger, and shares his thoughts on what the movie means to him.

Black Panther Movie Special: **How familiar were you with Marvel Comics before taking on your** *Black Panther* **role?**
Michael B Jordan: I was a big Marvel fan, growing up. I read the comics and graphic novels and watched the cartoons as a kid, so I was pretty familiar with the Marvel universe.

Were you familiar with the Black Panther character?
Very much so. He was a childhood favorite and a character that I always looked up to and admired. Black Panther was actually always a character that I wanted to play one day when I was a kid.

What did you like about Black Panther?
Being a person of color, being African-American and not having many Super Hero characters that look like me that I can actually relate to – he was the character I wanted to play. And I really fell in love with Wakanda, this world where black people were so strong and powerful.

How excited were you about Marvel Studios doing a Black Panther movie?
Oh, super excited. The character did so well in *Captain America: Civil War* – he pretty much stole a lot of the movie, in my opinion. Chadwick did such an amazing job playing him – it was only a matter of time before he got his own movie.

What appealed to you about this film?
Me and Ryan Coogler are like brothers. This is our third film together. This is a project that we spoke about, and he mentioned me coming on and doing something different, playing a villain. To be able to team up with him again was a no-brainer. And I haven't had the opportunity to work with Chadwick before, so this is great.

Tell us about your character.
I play Erik Killmonger. He's the villain of this film – but hopefully you can empathize with him and see where he's coming from. He has reasons for doing what he's doing and he feels that he's right. He's a very, very smart guy. He's very intelligent.

He went to MIT, graduated top of his class, enrolled in the Navy SEALs and special forces, and black ops. ▶

ERIK KILLMONGER – A BRIEF COMIC BOOK HISTORY

A deadly nemesis of the Black Panther, Erik Killmonger is an expert martial artist with genius-level intellect. The character was created by writer Don McGregor and artist Rich Buckler, and first appeared in *Jungle Action* #6 in 1973. Erik Killmonger is a terrifying match for T'Challa in wit and fighting skills, and his main goal is to return Wakanda to its cultural roots.

▶ **What's your character's look?**
Oh man, the look is awesome. Killmonger in the comics had really long hair, but this is a more modern version. The clothes are very urban but high-end fashion. He has good taste! We had a really good time picking clothes for him. He has a lot of sacrificial marks on his body for all the kills that he's gotten over the years. All the killing that he's doing is for a reason – it's not senseless. He believes what he's doing is right. So the sacrificial marks on his body are a constant self-reminder to be focused and to continue the mission straight through.

> "The physicality of this film is something I was really looking forward to. It's been fun – knife training, gun training, and the combat stuff."

What about your mask?
It was beautiful. I saw some mock-ups of it and I was so looking forward to wearing it. It just gets you in a certain mood. It really stands out and it's definitely a piece that I'm trying to take home with me! (*Laughs*)

How has your stunt-training been?
I love it. The physicality of this film is something I was really looking forward to. *Creed* was the first project where I really had to transform myself physically into something else.
    I did a year and a half of boxing training to sell that I was a real boxer. So to be able to

01 Erik Killmonger: ready for battle!

02 Jordan in Erik Killmonger's full outfit

03 Face to face with T'Challa

01

transform myself into Killmonger was fun. We have the same fight co-ordinator from *Creed* – Clayton J. Barber – so there's a shorthand there as well. It's been fun – knife training, gun training, and the combat stuff.

What was your reaction to the script?
My initial reaction was "Wow!" I think they did a really good job of laying down the foundation of Wakanda and introducing that world.

I loved the way they tied in the old school tradition and history with modern foreign policy – I think it's super important. They laid down a lot of tropes in there that I think are very smart and progressive. I'm very proud to be a part of this project. Ryan's always had that gift to be ahead of the curve and just be real and honest.

Why is this story important now?
I feel like it's inspiring to black people. It's not your stereotypical ▶

"I feel like *Black Panther* is not your stereotypical film. It's raw and it's real. It has real emotions and real feelings and real issues that we're addressing in a fantastic way."

film. It's raw and it's real. It has real emotions and real feelings and real issues that we're addressing in a fantastic way.

I feel like *Black Panther* needed its story told and I think the fans are owed that. It's definitely different than a lot of other Marvel films because the cast is predominantly black but super diverse at the same time.

What do you like so much about Ryan Coogler's process?
It's the honesty. He finds the real moments and real characters in whatever he works on, no matter how sci-fi or fantastical the world may be. Also, he's not a safe director. He's willing to take risks and I think that's important. There

are certain people you just click with. The first time I met him it was like I'd known him my whole life. We've become very close. Our shorthand on set is crazy!

How did you find working with Chadwick Boseman?
I've known him since I was about 17 back in New York, but this is my first time actually getting on set with him. Every time we saw each other we'd say we'll work together one day. So it was really cool and fun to actually see that come to life.

What's it like joining a Marvel Studios movie?
It's a dream come true, which might sound cheesy but it's something that

I've always wanted to do. And to be able to do it at this level with this director, with this studio, with this cast... it's lined up perfectly.

What separates *Black Panther* from the other films from Marvel Studios?
It takes risks and I feel like it's speaking to the world as it is today. It's also giving black people something to be very proud of and able to relate to and identify with.

The story's very honest and gritty. Whatever you'd expect from a Ryan Coogler film, that's what you're gonna get on this one, mixed in with what Marvel does so well. It has a lot of the right ingredients to make something really special. ∎

04 Erik Killmonger takes up arms as he challenges T'Challa to a fight

05 Erik Killmonger squares off against T'Challa's bodyguards, the Dora Milaje

LUPITA NYONG'O IS
NAKIA

Gracing the Marvel Cinematic Universe as the warrior Nakia, Oscar-winning actress Lupita Nyong'o talks about what it's like fighting in the world of Black Panther...

Black Panther Movie Special: What appealed to you about working on this movie?
Lupita Nyong'o: I had wanted to work with Ryan Coogler, so when I found out he was directing this film I was super excited. Plus, of course, Black Panther was Marvel's first black Super Hero and now he is going to be on the big screen! Also, the fact that we were going to be creating this really dope African country that everyone would want to be a part of was extremely exciting.

What has it been like, working with Ryan Coogler?
Ryan is incredible to work with. He throws himself into a project – you can tell by the amount of hair that grows on his face and his head while he's working! He's really into it. He used to be a football player, and he brings that to how he directs. It's like he's a coach, and we are his team. We're all working together toward a goal.

Tell us about your character.
Nakia is a bit of a rebel, but she's also a loyalist for her country. She is in conflict with some of the ideals of her nation and wants to go her own way. But she is also really eager to serve the country she loves so much. T'Challa and Nakia are at odds as to what the way forward is for the nation, but they also have some history together. They have to come to terms with that and figure out how to forge ahead.

How did you connect with your character?
I definitely connected with Nakia's free spirit and her independence. I love a woman who wants to do her own thing and has her own voice. I connected with her desire to want to do her own thing but also with her feeling of connection, responsibility, and a need for friends and family.

What is Nakia's connection to T'Challa?
T'Challa and Nakia have been friends for the longest time, and they also have a bit of a romantic past. Some of those feelings may still be in existence when we meet them. If they were on Facebook, their relationship status would be: "It's complicated."

What is your character's connection to Okoye?
Okoye and Nakia have a sisterhood, but it's challenged because Nakia doesn't do so well with authority figures, while Okoye doesn't do so well with rebels. Okoye represents the old guard and tradition. She's really eager to keep tradition alive, while Nakia challenges tradition. They have a deep respect for each other, but they see the world differently.

How is it working with Danai Gurira as Okoye?
I love Danai. I've been in a play that she wrote, and our sisterhood goes way back. It was lovely to bring that kind of relationship and the love we have for each other ▶

01

▶ to these characters who are trying to find their footing together and trying to cope with the different ways that they see each other. It was so much fun to finally work with her on screen.

What's it like to play such a fierce warrior?
I think that Nakia was born to be a warrior. She was born with a warrior spirit. Being the top warrior of her tribe is something that brings her a lot of pride and she's eager to make her people proud.

How was the stunt training?
The stunt training was intense, to say the least, but as I got my ass kicked, I felt more connected

"If T'Challa and Nakia were on Facebook, their relationship status would be: 'It's complicated.'"

to Nakia's warrior spirit. She is a woman that has traveled the world, and so her fighting style is informed by her experiences in the world.

Ryan described her style as street, while the Dora Milaje have a more graceful, traditional style of fighting. Nakia fights by any means necessary, so there was a little bit of Judo and Jiu-Jitsu and Filipino Martial Arts,

Capoeira, and Muay Thai all thrown in there.

What about the production values?
The production values of this movie are spellbinding. I remember once coming on set on a day that I wasn't called, and there was a tribal council scene being shot. It gave me

goosebumps because, for me, this was the image of what an African nation could have been if its development was left to itself. And there it was before us. It was just so inspiring.

Is this story an important one to tell now?
I think we could all use an awakening of our imaginations. Wakanda is something to aspire to. I feel right now the world is in a moment where we could really use some rejuvenation and some inspiration. What I love about Wakanda is that it's a country where anyone in our world, as we know it, can become a citizen if you just buy into the imagination of it. And that is powerful, especially now. ■

LETITIA WRIGHT IS
SHURI

Making her debut in the Marvel Cinematic Universe,
Letitia Wright explodes onto the screen as Black Panther's
genius sister, Shuri.

Black Panther Movie Special: What was your initial exposure to the Marvel universe?
Letitia Wright: My initial exposure was mainly through the films. As I started to look into the world of Black Panther I realized that it was a huge world in the Marvel Cinematic Universe, and there are different characters and different segments that intertwine.

What appealed to you about the project?
What appealed to me about it was the fact that we're exploring a Super Hero who is from Africa – so that was the first thing that I

immediately knew was going to be be fresh and different. I wanted to be a part of that.

What did you like about the script?
I liked it a lot because it had a balance of action and real emotions and things that people can also connect to. If you go to see films and it's just all about fighting, you can sometimes be detached. But this has a nice balance of exploring the emotions of the characters and family, and what it means to rule a nation, what it means to have that responsibility on your back, and how someone can deal with that and still protect his nation.

Tell us a bit about Shuri.
Shuri is the princess of Wakanda and also T'Challa's little sister. She's very intelligent and innovative. She's always creating stuff, and she designs all of the technology and the exciting, cool things that we're going to see in the film. Her brain is always ticking away and she's always thinking of solutions to help her country. I would like to say that Shuri is the heart of the film.

Did you have to do stunt training?
Yes, I did. We would do stunt training every day. It was tough! And any time I felt like I couldn't do it, they would push me forward and say "You can!" If you want to be someone that's a warrior you have to have a warrior's mentality and body and strength. I was ready to try out different armor and different weapons because they gave us that confidence. It's been cool.

What are Shuri's hopes for T'Challa?
Her hope is that he can be the king he wants to be. We meet our heroes in the midst of a hard time. We've just lost our father, King T'Chaka, and we have to make a transition into a new era. Shuri wants T'Challa to improve and take Wakanda into its next phase, and she wants to be right there alongside him, to help in whatever way she can.

> **What's the dynamic with their mother, Ramonda?**
The way they're dealing with it, this tragedy has happened, but Ramonda shields her children from it. She doesn't show them that side that's hurting. She tries to suppress it and move forward and support her child, T'Challa, in this new difficult phase that he's going through.

What was it like to have Angela Bassett play your mother?
Amazing! She did a movie called *Akeelah and the Bee* and it inspired me to want to do acting, so I told her that. And from that day onward, it's been a blast. When she sees things are going wrong for me on set or I'm having a frustrating time, she'll pull me to one side and be like, "Hey, you've got this." I'm honored to be working with her.

01 Letitia Wright as Shuri with co-star Lupita Nyong'o as Nakia

02 Technology expert Shuri at work

"I came in with an approach to be very serious, but Ryan Coogler let me know that Shuri needed to be the love and the light of the film."

What conversations did you have with Ryan Coogler about your approach to the character?
From the very start, Ryan let me know how he wanted me to play Shuri. I came in with an approach to be very serious and very strong, but Ryan let me know that Shuri needed to be the love and the light of the film. He was like, "Hey Tish, smile, be happy, encourage your brother and the people around you." Because of her age,

people can easily underestimate Shuri. When she opens her mouth about technology, it's like, "Oh, whoa, okay. You're really smart!" And I've had to just embrace that.

What's your character's look?
Shuri wears a lot of bright colors, and odd shapes, cuts, and designs. It's a mixture of tribal and youthfulness. She creates her own path when it comes to fashion and style. She wears what she loves. It

02

SHURI – A BRIEF COMIC BOOK HISTORY

A relatively recent addition to the Black Panther universe, Shuri, T'Challa's younger sister, first appeared in *Black Panther* Vol. 4 #2 in 2005. Always envious of her brother's title, she took on the responsibility of ruling Wakanda as princess while he was away fighting with the Fantastic Four. Shuri was an extensively trained martial artist, and defended her people from various threats. Eventually, she took on the trials and earned the title and powers of the Black Panther herself, imbued with strength, durability, and speed, while also obtaining her own vibranium uniform.

could be an odd shape, bright colors, cool rings. She's just a cool kid.

What's it like to be part of a film featuring such strong women?
It's brilliant. And that stemmed from the comic book, and the writers putting women at the forefront. You always see men as bodyguards for a king or whatever. But you have a king in a comic book whose circle is filled with women, and his advisors are also women. It's brilliant for the filmmakers to respect that.

What's it like to work with such an esteemed cast?
It's almost like a masterclass for me. I'm so humbled by it. I'm just learning so much from all of them. I watched these people for years and studied their work. When you see people on TV or at a red carpet event, you have your own ideas as

to who they are. But when I've been able to have real conversations, I've been able to see that they are real people, and they just love their job, and they're very talented.

Why is it important to tell this story now?
It's needed because we have to see, especially in Africa, more positive projections. And I think it's so important to give exposure to the different cultures that are filled throughout the whole continent. It's refreshing. And we want people to feel proud and happy about it.

What was it like shooting the Warrior Falls scene?
It was amazing. I've never been on a set like that before, and I'm already starting to miss it. The drums are playing, and as a people we're moving, we're dancing, we're singing. It was brilliant for me to

see, because it educated me to see that there's a root of where we come from. It's the heart and soul of the world.

What will separate this film from other Super Hero films?
There's so much depth to it. I had to remind myself that this is an action film because we've had so many scenes that are filled with such depth and richness. Plus showing people and tribes and cultures of Africa that we've not seen before – that's going to be amazing.

What experience are you hoping audiences will take from this?
I hope it's something that just touches their hearts. Yes, there's action and all of that good stuff. But there are also moments in this film that are heartfelt. So I hope they can take away the emotions and excitement of everything. ■

ANGELA BASSETT IS

RAMONDA

Angela Bassett brings a strong presence to *Black Panther*, playing the screen mother of T'Challa and Shuri. Here, the award-winning actress discusses her role as Ramonda.

Black Panther Movie Special: What was your initial exposure to Marvel Comics?
Angela Bassett: Not very much. I do have a friend who's a fan, though – Samuel L. Jackson! Lupita [Nyong'o] is going to pass her comic books on to me, so I'm looking forward to getting myself up to speed.

I had heard of Black Panther, but I wasn't familiar with the comic. So many people are excited about this film – he really is a popular and beloved character.

What initially appealed to you about the project?
I'm a big fan of Chadwick's work – the films that he has done. He just goes all in. I appreciate his body of work and his expertise, and Lupita and Michael B. Jordan are wonderful talents. But also there was the opportunity to work with Ryan Coogler – I'm such a big fan of his work – of *Creed* and *Fruitvale Station*.

This is a brand new world for me, the Marvel universe – the comic book world. It's different for me and I love being part of it.

Tell us about your character.
I'm Ramonda, the queen mother of Wakanda – and also Black Panther's mother. I'm the widow of T'Chaka. For years I've been asked what dream role I've always wanted to play – and I would say a queen!

How did you connect with this role?
Ramonda is a wife and the mother of a son of whom she is immensely proud. And she has a young daughter, Shuri, and they have that back and forth between mother and daughter as she's growing into adulthood.

There are different dynamics and tensions that play out between mothers and sons and mothers and daughters. I'm a mother myself, so I understand the relationship and the hopes and the aspirations that you have with them. Knowing what their challenges are, trying to support them, and helping them out of the nest.

What did the death of Ramonda's husband, T'Chaka, do to the family?
It brought them together – we drew closer to each other – and yet we still must reign. The entire country is still looking up to them. And it's the people's loss as well – he was the father of this nation. In African nations, the mother is the mother of all.

What were your initial conversations with Ryan Coogler about your character like?
Ryan is very collaborative and allows you to bring to it what you want. He asked us to ground our characters in our bodies, in our emotions, in our feelings, in reality, as opposed to a comic book and a character. It's about who these people are and how they feel about each other and what they want.

Ryan is full of passion and feeling. He wears his heart on his sleeve – and he listens. He greets everyone every day with a hug and a kiss, and he listens to your point of view and will take it into consideration.

He's hard-working. I don't know if he ever slept because he was always on the move and on it. He knew the script, the characters, and the story intimately. I appreciate him in every single way. ▶

01

▶ **What did you think of the script?**
It's about relationships and people and how they change and grow and interact. This Marvel Cinematic Universe is so huge and it really looks like magic to me.

What did you think of Chadwick's portrayal of T'Challa?
I thought it was a wonderful introduction – very centered, grounded, and strong – but there's still a mystery about him. Chadwick brings a warmth and camaraderie, and I looked at him with proud eyes, as his character's mother and also as a colleague, and as Angela.

And how about Letitia, who plays your on-screen daughter?
Letitia and I formed a very beautiful bond. She is a lovely young woman who is full of just fieriness and sass and humor and openness. I had a wonderful experience with her. We talked and conversed, and listened and learned from each other.

> **"For years I've been asked what dream role I've always wanted to play – and I would say a queen!"**

What's it like working with such an esteemed cast?
This cast is from all over the world, and it has been amazing. We have really become a family in a sense. We've spent hours on the set working very hard in the cold, in the heat, in these climates that baffled us from time to time.

But we also had time to go and break bread together and make music, and create laughter, experiences, and memories together. We've gone bowling, we've gone clubbing, and I know we've made friendships that will last a lifetime because we all have a sense that we've done something special here.

It's been hard work, but it's been so fulfilling, and we know that it's a world that audiences are waiting with bated breath to see.

What experience do you hope this film delivers?
I hope that it'll be satisfying for the fans, that their expectations of this world will be met. And I hope that it resonates with people who, like me, will go into it and become new fans. I hope the story, the relationships, and the themes will resonate just as powerfully for them as well.

How was the experience overall?
It was absolutely stunning and amazing. It was one of the best experiences in my career – in my life.

What parts of the movie are you most looking forward to seeing?
All of it! ■

01 Angela Bassett on set as Wakanda's queen, Ramonda, with her on-screen son T'Challa, played by Chadwick Boseman

02 Ramonda wields a ring blade

03 A royal family: Shuri and Ramonda

DANAI GURIRA IS

DANAI GURIRA IS
OKOYE

For Danai Gurira, playing Okoye, the head of the Dora Milaje, gave her the opportunity to explore notions of tradition, commitment, and responsibility – as well as giving her the chance to go toe-to-toe with Erik Killmonger. Moreover, the *Walking Dead* star was thrilled to participate in an African story on such an epic scale...

Black Panther Movie Special: What initially appealed to you about this project?

Danai Gurira: I loved the notion of making an African story on this type of scale. I'm from theater. I'm a playwright – I write about African stories and try to tell them in the Western context. So to see African characters put on an epic platform is something that you yearn for. To see this type of story get brought to light, and meeting with Ryan Coogler and hearing his vision – I was just extremely happy that it was happening at all. The fact that I could be a part of it as well was really amazing.

Tell us about your character.
Okoye is the head of the Dora Milaje. In the comic book, there are so many different renditions of the Dora Milaje. In our rendition, which is really cool, these women have pledged their lives to the throne – to the maintenance, the security of

the kingdom, and specifically of the throne.

In the case of my character, Okoye is the general of the armed forces as a whole and the head of [Black Panther's] intel. She's more than just the bodyguard – she's got a much more expansive role. She's deeply involved with all the workings of what's going on in the kingdom and she knows everything. She reports to T'Challa. She makes decisions and she's very well known for her abilities as a soldier and as a leader, and that's been very cool to play.

What does it mean to have that role in Wakanda?
She holds the role with great reverence. She's a huge traditionalist. She really, really believes in how her country was designed by her forefathers and foremothers, and she believes in maintaining that at all costs. She bears that weight every day. And, of course, maintaining the

security of the throne is a very big part of that.

So Okoye has an astounding pride in being Wakandan, and she also has a great love for her people. She goes to Busan to take out the enemy, she protects the king, she keeps track of all their war dogs – all of those things are about securing this nation's stability. She wants to take care of that little girl out there in the merchant tribe, or that little girl out there in the mining tribe who will then come out and be future leaders.

Describe Okoye's relationship with T'Challa.
Her connection to T'Challa is very close. They're good friends. They've grown up around each other. She was definitely a young girl who stood out from a young age from the border tribe. When she was being brought through the ranks she was close by him, so she's known T'Challa for a long time. You meet them both in the same scene at the same time, and ▶

understanding of his point of view, which makes him a very complex villain, which I think is the best type of villain, because a villain who just likes to be evil is really kind of boring.

The thing that's really great about Killmonger is that there is a point of view that he has about the experience of people of color, the experience of people of African descent. It's personal, it's very political and epic, his perspective, which I think is the best type of character.

Okoye and the Dora Milaje have a unique fighting style…
The Dora way of fighting is really beautiful. It was supposed to be inspired a little bit by a way of moving as one. In a way, it's almost dance-like. There were a lot of very interesting formations that we created, for instance when the Dora work together to take somebody down, or the fight we have with Killmonger. We were able to find a beautiful grace in these women, and also a ferocity. I think that's a really great combination.

What experience do you hope this film delivers?
You're gonna get your beautiful, out-of-this-world, amazing Super Hero movie. And then you're also gonna get something that feels really on the pulse of where we are right now as a global society. ■

► she's all up in his business, basically. They have a great relationship.

There is something that they're dealing with, which is the loss of his father. I think that's something that definitely affects her as well, because she's the head of the Dora Milaje. So the loss of the king is something that weighs hard on her heart as well. She has a deep sense of protection for T'Challa.

What's the connection to Nakia?
That's the business she's all up in, of course – the idea of T'Challa going to obtain Nakia. It's taken a while to find her, which is something that's on Okoye, because Nakia went so deep undercover. But that's Nakia. That's her power, which Okoye respects – that she's someone who gets so committed to her mission that she'll go to whatever lengths. But sometimes that can involve

> "The loss of the king is something that weighs hard on Okoye's heart as well."

loss of protocol. So it just took us a while to find her. We didn't find her in time for the funeral.

What's your take on Erik Killmonger? Will the audience sympathize with him?
I think Killmonger is a very, very fascinating character in a lot of ways. I think there will be an

01 Danai Gurira as Okoye in full warrior mode in the Busan scenes

02 Danai Gurira on the Busan set with Chadwick Boseman and Lupita Nyong'o

FLORENCE KASUMBA IS
AYO

Having already portrayed Ayo in *Captain America: Civil War*, Florence Kasumba says she loved getting to interact with the rest of the Dora Milaje in *Black Panther*.

Black Panther Movie Special: **What's it like to play such a powerful woman?** **Florence Kasumba:** What I love about it is it's the first time that I actually get to play a Super Hero. You have to be a woman in order to become one of the Dora Milaje. No man can become a Dora. You need to be extremely good because we are stronger than all the other people, like the king's guard, for example, or the border tribe.

Did you have to learn a particular fighting style for *Black Panther*?
I already came with a certain martial arts background, but I had to learn to work with my weapon. I'm working with a spear. Back home I do kung fu, but this is the first time that I'm actually working with a spear. So we did basic drills.

What's this experience been like?
I love working with the director. I love working with my colleagues; working with the Doras is so much fun because I'm working with strong women. Everybody has their own specialty. What I liked was I could go to my colleagues and say, "Hey, how would you do this kick? Would you do this?" We all just help each other. There are some people that could turn fast. There were people that could jump very well. It was just fine to exchange, experience, and teach each other, and listen.

What will make this film stand apart from other Super Hero films?
I was very moved by the story. What I like about this movie is we have a Super Hero who is also a leader of a country. And we have this beautiful country with beautiful people. You will find out about the history of this country and the traditions. These are things that I haven't seen in other Super Hero movies.

CONCEPT ART

Okoye, Shuri, and the Dora Milaje face an unusual foe.
Art by Vance Kovacs

ANDY SERKIS IS

ULYSSES KLAUE

He's been an actor, producer, and director – and now Andy Serkis can add Marvel Studios supervillain to his list! Here, Andy discusses his approach to taking on one of Marvel Comics' classic characters...

Black Panther Movie Special: **Ulysses Klaue first appeared in Marvel Studios'** Avengers: Age of Ultron **– how was your experience on that movie?**
Andy Serkis: Interestingly, the way I got involved in all this was the Imaginarium, which is our performance capture studio in London. Joss Whedon came to have a look and said, hey, do you want to come and play a character? And I said I'd love to do that. Then Ulysses Klaue was set to appear, and Joss said, "We'd love you to play that." So I was very excited, and I loved his scene. It was really witty. He was quite a funny character – very dark but comedic as well.

What appealed to you about Black Panther**?**
I really love the Black Panther character in the comics. And Ulysses Klaue comes into the fore in a strong way in this story. Then when I heard Ryan Coogler was doing it, I just thought, wow, that's

amazing. I think he's a brilliant director. He's just such an extraordinary force on set, a really natural leader without having to be over-authoritative. He's all about character. He knows this world so well. It's been real fun. And he allows you to come up with ideas, which has been great.

Where do we find Klaue this time around?
Klaue has mercenary teams that work with him all over the world and he has heard that there is some vibranium in the British Museum. Klaue is addicted to vibranium, so he goes to get it. He knows how much it's worth...

How do you connect with the character?
I think it's his internal sense that he's getting what he justly thinks he deserves. When you're playing characters, you have to believe that their moral compass is in alignment with yours. I think one

of the things I've really tried to hold onto is his sense of wanting to unearth and expose hypocrisy.

What's the importance of vibranium?
It's perceived that only a tiny amount of it exists, but what we actually reveal in this film is that there is a huge amount of vibranium. It's making [Wakanda] the wealthiest country in the world. So the fact that it's hidden and kept for its own country and is unexploited by the rest of the world is quite an extraordinary thing.

What do you think of Chadwick Boseman's portrayal of T'Challa?
I just think he's incredible. I mean his discipline, his focus; he brings a lot of gravitas to the role. It feels very believable, emotionally very truthful. You can see he's conflicted. And, you know, he's an amazing physical performer and a great martial artist too. Some of the stuff that he's had to do on this has been absolutely unbelievable in terms of the fighting. ▶

What was your initial reaction to the script?

I thought Ryan had come up with something really special. It was a really extraordinary retelling of everything that we know about Black Panther, and of creating Wakanda in the way that he has and putting that emphasis there. I just think the script is really smart, really skillful and very pertinent to our times.

What initial conversations did you have with Ryan?

We wanted [Ulysses] to carry on being an arms dealer but also to be in touch politically with governments and so forth. I wanted Ulysses Klaue to have that anger

that he feels towards [Wakanda] based on the fact that he was kind of brutalized there, and the fact that they are actually pretending to be something that they're not. If there is a redeeming factor about Ulysses Klaue, it's that he would want to expose hypocrites, whether in government or a power or a country.

What do you like most about Ryan Coogler's directorial process?

He's just so incredibly collaborative and allows you to try stuff – he *dares* you to try stuff. For every single take, he'll have an idea, or if you come up with an idea he'll bounce off that.

01 Andy Serkis returns to the Marvel Cinematic Universe as the mercenary, Ulysses Klaue

02 A captured Klaue is interrogated by Everett K. Ross

03 Serkis was happy to be reunited with his *Hobbit* and *Captain America: Civil War* co-star, Martin Freeman

> "Having a story that focuses on a black Super Hero is so important. It's crazy that there hasn't been one up to now."

ULYSSES KLAUE – A BRIEF COMIC BOOK HISTORY

Ulysses Klaue was created by comic legends Stan Lee and Jack Kirby as an enemy of the Black Panther. He first appeared in 1966 in *Fantastic Four* #53, as the son of a Nazi war criminal who became a physicist in the field of applied sonics. Having lost his right arm stealing the rare metal vibranium from Wakanda, and killing the king, Black Panther's father, In the process, he became the supervillain Klaw, capable of manipulating sound for complete destruction. He even became a being entirely composed of sound waves, ironically his only weakness being vibranium.

What's been your reaction to the sets?

It's just incredible. The detail on the sets is phenomenal. They're beautifully crafted. The Korean fish market was unbelievable, and the casino itself was absolutely extraordinary. Every single set has been just world class.

How's the casino shoot been?

It was a great scene to shoot. It was fantastic, and I've really enjoyed working with Martin Freeman again [reprising his role as Everett K. Ross, last seen in *Captain America: Civil War*]. We had an enormous amount of fun playing those scenes.

It's a pretty spectacular affair with a huge stunt sequence and actually some of the most brilliant physical stunts I've witnessed on camera – especially when T'Challa gets hit with the sonic blaster and goes flying! The stuntman just did this most amazing flip backwards and landed on a table. It was extraordinary to watch.

Why is it important to tell the Black Panther story now?

Because we are living in such a polarized world that is driven by super capitalism. Having the really great, diverse cast that we do, having a great story that focuses on a black Super Hero, it's so important. It seems crazy that there hasn't been one up to now. And, you know, this is the first film of its kind.

What ride will the audience get out of this?

It's a thriller. It's dramatic. It's emotional at times, and it has a historical aspect that is very rare. So it has an epic quality to it and a mythological kind of quality to it. ■

MARTIN FREEMAN IS
EVERETT K. ROSS

Making his Marvel Studios debut in *Captain America: Civil War*, CIA operative and the Deputy Task Force Commander of the Joint Counter Terrorist Centre Everett K. Ross is back. Actor Martin Freeman discusses his return to the role in *Black Panther*...

**Black Panther Movie Special: What initially appealed to you about this film? What was your reaction to the script?
Martin Freeman:** The script was more political than I thought it might be, in a way that I like. It seemed to be getting things that we've been having conversations about for many, many years but aren't often hinted at in Super Hero movies.

My take on it was very positive. I like Ryan [Coogler] as well. I've seen his previous work and liked it. So I had faith and trust in him. But it's not like a dry political treatise. It's still a Super Hero movie. But I think, for a Super Hero movie, it's pretty political, and pretty timely.

It's a relevant story.
I think the points that I'm talking about have been relevant for ages.

And certainly the world is, and when we say the world, what do we really mean? Britain and America. Those two countries in the world, which constitute the world, are in a state of high flux at the moment. And everything seems to be up for grabs. There are specific things in this movie that hint at that. There are specific references in this movie about bridges instead of walls and opening up borders, which is not going to be lost on anybody, I don't think. But it's not done in a worthy way of winking at the audience.

Where do we find Everett K. Ross this time around?
We find him in the middle of a job. He's about to do a deal with Ulyssess Klaue. He then sees that half of Wakanda are in the room, including T'Challa. And so he's thinking, *Okay, what are they doing here? They've not come to talk. They've come for potential business.* From Everett's point of view he is now in the middle of something that could go off very badly, and indeed it does go off very badly!

What was Ross' intent when asking T'Challa to stay out of things?
I think Ross is very good at his job, and he trusts the 15 or so people he's got with him to stick to the script: this is gonna happen with Klaue. There is another whole element as the good people of Wakanda come in. That is not part of his plan at all. These people are not librarians. They're people who are capable of great violence. So that's not good news for Ross. He's not an actual Super Hero. He can't knock buildings over. He can get killed, and there are 150 people in that casino who could all get killed as well. So I think I'm ▶

01

> "I'm trusting that Everett K. Ross is a reasonably good guy, and he doesn't want to see loads of innocent people get killed."

02

trusting that he's a reasonably good guy, Everett, and he doesn't want to see loads of innocent people get killed.

What did you think of Chadwick Boseman's portrayal in _Civil War_?
I thought he was great! He's got a great stillness to him where you can kind of believe he is of noble birth. There are things about him that are quite conservative and quite held back, which is always good because you want to see more from those characters. If someone comes out and it's all at 10 then there's nowhere else to go, whereas with his portrayal you knew there was a lot more to see, a lot more layers to unpeel.

What's it like working with the special effects?
The first time around, it's exhilarating because there's a lot of noise going on around you. Inwardly you're going, _Oh, wow, it's not even exciting._

I have to not mess this up because if I mess this up then there's a lot of reset! Fortunately it was hardly a scene about Everett K. Ross. He was a very small component. But I'm very aware of being technically just on point and trying to not mess it up because there are a thousand other pieces to that jigsaw puzzle.

What did you think of the realization of Wakanda?
The aesthetics on this film and the visuals on this film have been incredible and a real pleasure to watch and to wear the stuff. But, obviously, Everett doesn't wear the most outlandish gear in the film. There are people who are pushing the boat out a little bit more than he is. But just look at what people are wearing, look at the hair, look at the makeup, look at the scarification, the ornaments on people's faces and in ears. It's pretty amazing. ■

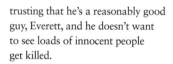

01 Martin Freeman returns to the Marvel Cinematic Universe as Everett K. Ross

02 Freeman filming the interrogation scene with Andy Serkis. The two previously worked together on *The Hobbit* trilogy and *Captain America: Civil War*

03 Sharing a scene with Chadwick Boseman

DANIEL KALUUYA IS

W'KABI

Red hot star Daniel Kaluuya talks about starring
as W'Kabi, T'Challa's oldest friend, in the latest Marvel
Studios Super Hero film to storm onto the big screen.

Black Panther *Movie Special*: **What appealed to you about the *Black Panther* movie?**
Daniel Kaluuya: Ryan Coogler being part of it and the cast they were assembling. I feel like Ryan is a director for the people – he makes movies for the people. This film has got buzz already. I've never seen such a reaction to me being cast in something like this! I think you always need more black role models and black figures. This is an African blockbuster in my eyes.

Is the film's timeliness why Marvel Studios decided to make it?
I think they're just plugged in. They're drawing from real life. They're not in their own industry bubble. They're looking around at what people are interested in and stories that people want to hear. And to have Ryan, who wants to be cinematic and wants to be big and wants to tell an honest, true, conflicting, complicated story – it's amazing.

Tell us about your character.
I play W'Kabi, who is T'Challa's oldest friend. He is the leader of the tribe who protects the border and makes sure that Wakanda is kept a secret.

What did you connect with in the character?
The fact that he's committed to the cause and is willing to do things that are a bit unpopular in order to do what's right. He's doing his job, even though a lot of people told him not to do it, because he believed in it. I really connected to that in W'Kabi.

What is his opinion about the state of Wakanda?
I think he feels Wakanda could be a great country, like a superpower. W'Kabi's ambitious, and he wants Wakanda to be as great as he knows it is.

What conversations have you had with Ryan Coogler?
Approach the character in the

sense of giving him nuances and complexities, especially in terms of his relationship with Okoye. What does it mean for Okoye and her work? That's a very modern argument. What does that do to the man in the relationship – when a woman is so committed to her job? W'Kabi is a traditionalist who wants to start a family and sees a woman's role as being at home.

These are badass women in this movie!
Yeah. And what does that do to a relationship, if your woman is a badass? Not many men can handle that, you know? That's a really honest comment.

Do you have a sense of Ryan Coogler's directing style?
He's very open and he listens, which is so nice. You feel like what you're bringing is valuable. I think he's very trusting of us in the sense that he wants us to guide our narrative alongside him as opposed to him telling us what to do. ▶

► Some of the cast worked with a dialect coach – how did that go?
It's been really intense getting a new dialect and wrestling with that and staying in character throughout the whole day. It's been really quite cool. But that's what I love about this job.

Describe your character's look.
Someone said I look like an African Jedi, and I feel like that was quite a good description. We wear these really big blankets, inspired by a South African tribe which Ryan went out there to research. Our hands are hidden but then the blanket comes off and W'Kabi's got knives and he's war ready. There's a duplicity of being humble and unassuming, but when it's fight time, the blanket comes off. We've got swords underneath, and weaponry, armor, everything. It's like a metaphor of Wakanda: it's hidden, but the inside reveals who you are.

What are the sets like?
They are epic. Warrior Falls was one of the best. When Chad emerges and everyone is singing and dancing and drumming – I thought, *this is gonna blow people's minds!* It wasn't done

01

"Someone said I look like an African Jedi, and I feel that was quite a good description!"

by CGI. We were there, and the vibe was there, and the water was there. When Chad came out for the first time I got goosebumps. Like, "wow, this is a moment!"

What will separate this film from other Super Hero films?
There's never been a Super Hero movie set in Africa. It's got an opportunity to say something real about the world and real about society and real about community.

And it's a majority black cast. Black people and Martin Freeman – what more do you want? And it has a lot of heart. That's the thing about Ryan – he has a lot of heart.

What's been most gratifying about working on this film?
For me, it's feeling like you're a part of something that's never been done before. That's what you do it for, and it's what makes it one of the most amazing experiences.

I remember they were drumming while we were doing the stunt training, and it was really exciting. I don't even see it as a film about diversity. I see it as just telling a world story. I think it's important to tell all our stories because we're an international market.

What do you hope this film delivers to audiences?
I want someone to get out of the cinema and run down the street for no reason! Do you ever have that moment where you're just like, "I need to do something"? You feel so empowered no matter where you come from, no matter who you are, no matter what your color is. It's just to feel empowered, whatever your political views, and feel: "I just experienced that. I'm with them, and I'm with this world." ∎

01 Daniel Kaluuya as W'Kabi

02 W'Kabi and Erik Killmonger

03 W'Kabi confers with Okoye

FOREST WHITAKER IS
ZURI

Award-winning actor Forest Whitaker has built up a huge résumé over the last 35 years, and now he can add Marvel Studios' *Black Panther* to his list, in which he plays Zuri. Here we review Whitaker's incredible career to date.

Born and raised in Longview, Texas, growing up, Forest Whitaker became a star quarterback before he made his way into college on a football scholarship. After an injury, he later transferred to the University of Southern California where he began to study opera and drama instead. During his time there he earned two more scholarships training as an operatic tenor. This led him to yet another scholarship at Berkeley, focusing on acting and performing on stage.

In 1982, at the age of 21, Whitaker made his film debut opposite Nicolas Cage and Sean Penn in the teen comedy *Fast Times at Ridgemont High*, playing a familiar role of a footballer. In his second film, 1985's *Vision Quest*, he played a student wrestler. In the early 80s he took on small TV roles in *Diff'rent Strokes*, *Cagney & Lacey,* and the civil war epic *North and South*. In 1986, he made a big impact with his performance in *The Color of Money*. This led to more film roles in *Platoon*, *Stakeout*, and *Good Morning, Vietnam*.

In 1988, Whitaker earned the leading role in Clint Eastwood's dark biopic *Bird* as the titular Charlie "Bird" Parker, an American jazz saxophonist and composer. For this role, Whitaker earned the Cannes Film Festival award for Best Actor. This role showcases Whitaker's reputation for thorough character studies into the parts he plays.

His roles can vary from meek, quiet characters, to prominent darker characters. His smaller role in the first part of 1992's *The Crying Game*, in which he played Jody, a kidnapped black British soldier, made a large impact on his career. The 90s then saw him take on leading and supporting roles in a variety of films, including *Diary of a Hitman* and *Ghost Dog: Way of the Samurai*.

The 90s also saw him producing and directing several films. In 1993, he directed the gritty HBO TV-film *Strapped*, for which he won the Toronto International Film Festival Critic's award. In 1995, he directed his first big screen film, *Waiting to Exhale*, based on the novel of the same name by Terry McMillan and starring Whitney Houston and Angela Bassett. During this time he also directed music videos, including Whitney Houston's "Exhale (Shoop Shoop)."

Whitaker was both the director and executive producer of the romantic comedy *First Daughter* with Katie Holmes and Michael Keaton. He produced multiple made-for-television movies through his production company, Spirit Dance Entertainment, including 2002's Emmy-award winning *Door to Door*, starring William H. Macy. He shut down his production company in 2005 to focus on his acting career, getting more roles in TV and film, including a recurring character in *The Shield*.

In 2006, Whitaker had one of his greatest successes so far, in *The Last King of Scotland*. He won several awards for his role in this film, including an Academy Award, British Academy Film Award, Golden Globe Award, National Board of Review Award, and a Screen Actors Guild Award. In the same year, the 10th Annual Hollywood Film Festival presented him with the "Hollywood Actor of the Year Award." He went on to win several other awards, including the Cinema for Peace Award 2007.

His acting portfolio expanded further in 2007 when he co-starred in *The Great Debaters* with Denzel Washington, and then acted opposite

Keanu Reeves in *Street Kings* the following year. That same year, he earned a star on the Hollywood Walk of Fame. 2009 saw Whitaker co-star in Spike Jonze's *Where the Wild Things Are*.

In more recent years he has taken on parts in several crime dramas, including *A Dark Truth* in 2012, and *The Last Stand* in 2013, in which he starred opposite Arnold Schwarzenegger. In 2013, he played the starring role in the Lee Daniels film *The Butler*.

In addition to his contributions to film and TV, Whitaker has done extensive humanitarian work, including working closely with charities that provide assistance to abused teenagers and animals. In recent years, he has become a spokesperson for Hope North Ugandan orphanage and Human Rights watch. 2001 saw him earn a Humanitas Prize.

In 2016, Whitaker took on the role of Saw Gerrera in *Star Wars: Rogue One*. He continued playing the role in the *Star Wars: Rebels* TV show. *Black Panther* in 2018 will be his debut role in the Marvel Cinematic Universe as Zuri, a Wakandan Shaman and trusted adviser to King T'Challa. ■

WINSTON DUKE IS
M'BAKU

Some characters change dramatically in their translation from comics to movies – and that is certainly true of M'Baku, who gets a contemporary update for the *Black Panther* film. Here, Winston Duke talks about his role, the language of his character, and his interesting experience in a comic shop…

Black Panther Movie Special: **What was your initial exposure to the Marvel comics and films?**
Winston Duke: I grew up reading the comic books. I read *X-Men*, watched cartoons like *Amazing Spider-Man*, dressed up in towels, things like that. I wasn't really deeply exposed to *Black Panther* in particular – that was more a fringe comic.

Did you do research into the character when you signed on for the movie?
I read the Reginald Hudlin issues, which kind of took more of a cinematic approach to the Black Panther tale. I got a lot of great juicy things from that. There was a lot of pride and strength and a really great world narrative of what Wakanda was, how they saw themselves and what separated them from the rest of the world in a really empowering way.

Also, the Marvel community and fans have been really, really helpful. I didn't tell anyone that I was cast as M'Baku and I went along to this really great comic book store in North Hollywood… The guy who owned the store just kept looking at me and smiling, and I was thinking, *well, I'm a good-looking guy…* He brought some books over to me and said, "I *know*…" I go, "What do you know?" He said, "I just know."

Then he just started telling me about the Marvel universe and Black Panther's narrative from when he was first being introduced in *Fantastic Four* up until the most recent Ta-Nehisi Coates iterations. He went through his entire stock and pulled out all the first appearances of M'Baku, and pretty much made a M'Baku list for me: every time he appeared in any comic book. So this guy kinda became my usher into seeing M'Baku in that comic bookscape. And it's that kind of generosity that I've been encountering from what I would call the Marvel community. These stories and narratives have meant so much to them. They've been able to see themselves in this.

What was your initial reaction to the *Black Panther* script?
My first response was that it was incredibly grounded. I loved how grounded all the stakes were and that this is essentially a family story: a nuclear family, a family in the sense of a communal family and a family in the sense of a cultural family.

Tell us about your character.
M'Baku is a self-professed man of deep integrity. He really cares about his people, and he's deeply shaped and defined by his cultural identity. He is Jabari, which is one of the main tribes of Wakanda. This is a really big part of who he is.

He has a particular way of wanting his world to reflect where he comes from. He does not want that to be forgotten.

What did you like about the character?
The conversations with Ryan Coogler have been about what Wakanda means to this man, and what his culture and his people mean to him. M'Baku loves them, they love him, and he's willing to die for that. There's something really powerful about that.

A really great thing about my relationship so far with Ryan is that he gave a lot of trust to me. He allowed me to create, and then we met in the middle. And we had beautiful conversations about how ▶

"M'Baku really cares about his people, and he's deeply shaped by his cultural identity."

▶ we could tell the best story. He trusts his actors, and we trust him. Working with Ryan also helped me to get to another level of understanding the character.

Working with Ryan and us having a deep sense of service to the story helped me to understand who M'Baku was. M'Baku's a man who has a great need to do a service for his people. He's serving something higher and bigger than himself.

He has to make sure that the Jabari survive and their ways and their culture survives, and that goes right back to us all wanting to make the best film. We're all serving this film.

How did the dialect coaching go?
That was fun. M'Baku has more of a Nigerian Igbo influence. It's not Igbo, but it's influenced by Igbo because the rest of the cast is doing South African Xhosa. So they're doing something very specific and rooted and grounded.

For M'Baku's mountain strong people, who have been sequestered in the mountains and have developed their own culture, we wanted something that had its own personality and its own beauty. So we referenced Igbo, and the rhythm of that language influenced the rhythm of my character.

Why *this* story now?
Because we need it. The world has changed. We're a lot more connected with the advent of social media connecting us in different ways. I can have a conversation with a person in Africa, the Caribbean, China – anywhere – about my ideas about the Marvel universe. And they can communicate with me easily. It's not that we're going to see this movie and then be disconnected. They're going to be able to interact with this. And they're going to see themselves represented on screen, and it's going to mean so much to them. This film will connect people.

What experience will the audience get?
I just hope that it's a brilliant experience. I just hope everyone has a chance to take it in and digest it and see what it means to them. ∎

M'BAKU – A BRIEF COMIC BOOK HISTORY

A frequent enemy of Black Panther, M'Baku is better known in the comics as Man-Ape, the second greatest warrior in Wakanda. He gained mystical powers by bathing in the blood, and eating the flesh, of the sacred Wakandan white gorilla, acquiring its strength, speed, stamina, agility, and durability. He also had extensive military training in hand-to-hand combat from the Wakandan militia. Man-Ape was created by Roy Thomas and John Buscema and first appeared in *Avengers* #62 in 1969. He has been affiliated with the Lethal Legion, Masters of Evil, and Villains for Hire.

01 Winston Duke as M'Baku

02 Stare wars! M'Baku fixes his gaze on his enemies

CONCEPT ART
Black Panther and M'Baku
square off! Art by J. Sweet

WELCOME TO
WAKANDA

From Wakanda's waterfalls and palaces to casinos in Busan and London's British Museum, the world of *Black Panther* is huge. Here, we take a sneak peek at some of the settings…

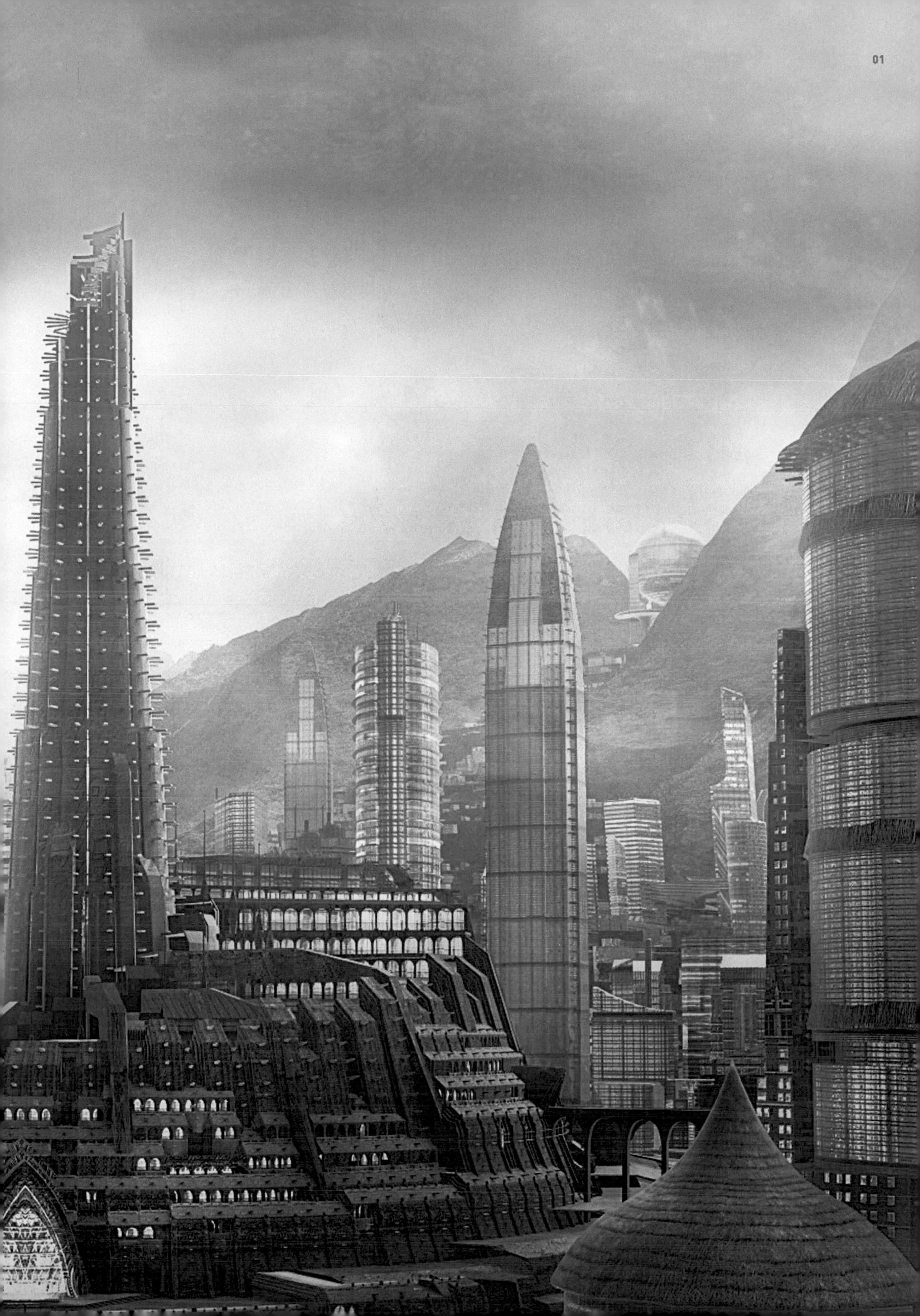

02

Production Designer Hannah Beachler: "Since Wakanda doesn't exist, it gave me a lot of freedom to create and go crazy! I really wanted to be thoughtful about the look of it – to take ideas from Kirby and bring them into the 20th Century, and use some of Ta-Nehisi's material as source as well. We also visited South Africa, and you can see what architecture of the future looks like there."

Executive Producer Nate Moore: "The cast really responds to sets that are as three-dimensional as possible. It helps them to really inhabit the characters, inhabit the world in a way that feels realistic. If we tried to do all this against a complete blue backdrop we wouldn't get the same kind of performance."

03

04

05

06

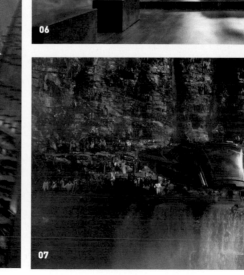

07

08

Production Designer Hannah Beachler: "For the tribal council room, we went for a circle of life idea, which is in a lot of tribal cultures, mixing the past and present together so the past is always there. We have a glass floor and there is old Nigerian lettering on the columns. One of the extras from Nigeria came in and said, 'I can read that story, I know what it says.'"

09

08 The Dora Milaje
on guard

09 The regal throne
room of the Wakandan
royal family

10 T'Challa takes to
his throne

ACTION!

Fight Coordinator Clayton J. Barber brings a wealth of Hollywood experience to *Black Panther*, not least his work on Ryan Coogler's previous movie, *Creed* (2015), which starred Michael B. Jordan. But stepping into the world of Wakanda gave him the opportunity to introduce audiences to a whole new set of fighting styles – ones he says the principal actors embraced wholeheartedly.

Black Panther Movie Special: You've worked with Ryan Coogler before – what do you like about his process, particularly in terms of the action scenes?
Clayton J. Barber: I like his attention to detail, and the fact that he listens to everything around him, trying to find creative inspiration. His passion also makes him special as a director. He works very closely with the fight guys, involving himself in the story and the choreography, and how it pertains to what he's trying to get on screen. I think that's what makes him really magical.

Take us through the biggest fight sequences in this film.
We have T'Challa fighting M'Baku, and then the waterfall fight where you see T'Challa fighting Killmonger. Then we have the great mountain stuff – your big finale where all the characters are fighting and everything's coming to a head. And then we have the casino fight, where T'Challa is vulnerable because he doesn't have his armor.

Which fighting styles will we see?
Going into this fictional universe of Wakanda, we had to try to approach what that would mean from an African sense of what African martial arts was. It's a very unique challenge, because you don't see this kind of action on film very often.
We took inspiration from all different sorts of fighting styles and amalgamated them into our own universe, trying to keep the integrity of, say, African movements such as Capoeira. You add a little bit of the Kali in there, and the Silat and movements like that. And you just try to watch the inspiration from the African rhythms and the beats, and you try to apply it to a universe we're trying to create. That was a very difficult challenge. We've found a compromise and balance to it, and hopefully it'll come off on screen. ▶

01 Black Panther hitches a ride through the streets of Busan

"We took inspiration from all different sorts of fighting styles."

Did you reference the comics in your research?

Everything starts there, from the characters' powers, to what they wear, how they act, who their parents are, where they were born... You get to use all of that in order to understand the experiences they gain. For instance, Killmonger has traveled the world and amassed all kinds of different styles of fighting.

A lot of the actors do their own stunts in this movie.

Yes – Chadwick, Michael, Danai, Lupita – they all trained for five months and they put their heart and soul into it. They're all very physical.

One of the things that I like to do as the fight coordinator is to push the actors to do the majority of things themselves. And if they can't or if we're doing something that's a little bit dangerous, then we put the stuntman in there. I personally like the actor to learn as much as they can – so they feel what it is they're going through physically. Even if they don't do it, then they can contribute to the stuntman who is doing it, saying this is how my character would be, and this is what I want you to do.

Did the cast have an idea of what they signed up for?

I don't think some of them did! But I have to tell you, there were zero complaints. They worked out, and you can see it in the performances. You can see it when Danai and Lupita are fighting in the casino. All that hard work comes across.

Chadwick is already a martial artist. He has a lot of experience and training – he had to learn to become physical for his roles. And Michael B. Jordan is an athlete. He's a boxer and he played basketball. He has a photographic memory, so you show him a piece of choreography and he's got it.

How do the costumes play into the fights?

We talk with every department – costumes, production design, art decoration, props – to make sure things are safe, right, and functional. We have to sometimes base our choreography around a certain costume. If T'Challa has a shield and he has to do a rolling move, sometimes you might not be able to do that. So we would replace a move with something that would fit.

How do you handle the safety of the extras?

We have a hundred extras and we have to pay attention to every one. You want to try to motivate them and encourage them to involve themselves in a scene, because the extras are feeding the energy to the actors playing the parts that are living the experience. The main actors that are fighting can feed off the energy. ■

02

03

02 Andy Serkis films one of the Busan action sequences as he unleashes his sonic weapon

03 Erik Killmonger caught between Shuri and Nakia

04 Like many of the *Black Panther* cast, Danai Gurira (Okoye) worked out to meet the demands of her role

COSTUMES

Both the Costume and Visual Development departments worked closely with director Ryan Coogler to develop an aesthetic for the Wakandans that embraced and celebrated diverse African cultures...

02

03

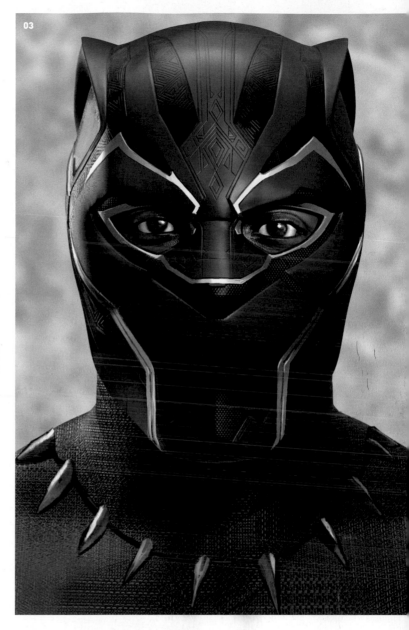

Ruth Carter, Costume Designer: "The new Black Panther suit is a Super Hero suit. We put a silver missile suit underneath it and made it out of a very thin fabric so that you could see his muscle patterns were made of vibranium. The *Civil War* suit felt a little bit more militaristic, thicker, and heavier – it was tougher. The new suit is a little bit more streamlined and can do a whole lot more with less.

"With a lot of the tribal patterns and prints there's a triangle pattern, so we put the triangle pattern all over his suit. It's called Okavango.

"Chadwick Boseman is easy to dress. He's a martial artist, so his physique is really good. He's the perfect specimen for dressing in clothes and also being a Super Hero."

01 Black Panther costume concept art by Ryan Meinerding

02 Chadwick Boseman in the final Black Panther costume, created by Ruth Carter and the Costume Department

03 Black Panther headshot, art by Adi Granov

04 Erik Killmonger's battle suit, concept art by Josh Nizzi

05 Michael B. Jordan as Erik Killmonger

06 Erik Killmonger's guerilla warfare suit

07 Erik Killmonger's tribal mask, art by Tully Summers

08 Erik Killmonger's "badass" battle suit

Ruth Carter, Costume Designer:
"Erik Killmonger's suit is incredibly special. One of our film's Panthers has a gold undertone, a gold-spotted suit, and the other is vibranium. We put this real gold suit underneath Erik Killmonger's skin suit, and he has a heavier gold necklace. He's a little bit more ostentatious than Panther. He's a little bit more street – I would say. It's a badass suit!"

09 Okoye (Danai Gurira) undercover

10 Okoye in her Dora Milaje clothing

11 Concept art for the Dora Milaje, T'Challa's personal bodyguards. Art by Anthony Francisco

Ruth Carter, Costume Designer: "The look of the Dora Milaje had to have some meaning and a cultural base. The harness is made of leather and if you look closely you'll see a lot of hand-stitching and a lot of beadwork. There's a buckle that has a cat face too – I felt like their harness is a thing that one Dora passes down through the generations. They have little talismans, little protection pieces, and I wanted the centerpiece to have a tribal meaning."

12 Shuri concept art
by Tully Summers

13

09 Concept art
for M'Baku wearing
his ape mask,
by Tully Summers

WARRIOR FALLS

Black Panther's Special Effects Coordinator Jesse Noel is no stranger to Marvel Studios – he also worked on *Captain America: Civil War* and *Avengers: Age of Ultron*. Here, Noel discusses the new challenges brought by *Black Panther* – in particular, keeping his head above 125,000 gallons of water on the Warrior Falls set…

01

Black Panther Movie Special: What attracted you to working on Black Panther?
Jesse Noel: What initially attracted me to working on the *Black Panther* movie was that I'd worked on *Captain America: Civil War* where he was introduced. He was a very cool, exciting character with his vendetta and everything that he was working towards. And it was something that I wanted to be a part of just because it looked very cool.

Naturally, there are a lot of ambitious special effects in *Black Panther*, but those centered around Warrior Falls seem of a different scale altogether...
Warrior Falls was one of the larger sets for us for this movie and one of the biggest things that we've been talking about since the very beginning. It's been one of the main staples that hasn't changed for us – its scope and everything attached to it as far as the special effects goes, with wind and water and taking care of the waterfalls, and having the pool be just right for the actors to be

able to fight in and be able to splash around in without too much splash. The waterfall's going in a way that you could see them and really have them in camera, but not have them be overpowered by sound and other reasons.

How did the filmmaking process start for you?
The process started for us when we had conceptual meetings about the Falls, and they'd built a small scale model and talked about where they were going to have the actual water parts, and where the pool was

01 Concept art for the Warrior Falls sequence, by Karla Ortiz

"I've worked on a few water sets, but nothing of this scope or magnitude."

going to be, where the water was going to drop down, and where it would spill over the front. Then we started talking about how we would actually fill it out mechanically, and how we would make it work to recirculate and make it a functional set for us.

What materials did you need to use because of the water element?
The construction department had built the set in a way that it was waterproof as well as having a soft space that the actors would be able to work with and be able to fight and slam each other down in without being injured. So underneath the water there was almost a foam surface that they'd be able to step and work around in.

How many waterfalls do we see?
In the Warrior Falls set there are four main waterfalls, and they're fed by six large pumps.

What are some of the problems associated with filmmaking with water?
One of the issues that we knew we were going to get into weather-wise was that when you have a water set, you want to heat it up to be warm and comfortable for everybody. But if you heat it up too much, steam will often start coming up if the weather's too cold. So that was sort of a battle for us, finding just the right temperature where it's comfortable for the actors without getting steam on the surface of the water.

How did you keep things safe?
One of the things that the stunt department had to do was fasten all the background actors to the set in the back. Construction had to build access for them to be able to step

in and go into their positions, and stunts had to go in and fasten each of them to the walls in the back of it.

How great is it shooting practically?
One of the things that is really nice about working with Marvel Studios is that they do have that practical aspect, that they like to get as much of it in camera as they can. It was exciting to be able to have them say, "build this," and we built it. The shots looked great. It was very exciting to have it all there, real, and in camera, and the actors actually fighting in the water and the waterfalls flowing.

How big were the tanks for Warrior Falls?
Warrior Falls itself is a recirculating system. We had six large submersible pumps that pumped the water up pipes and up to holding tanks; then

the water poured back down onto the set. And then it goes back down underneath to where it's recirculated again. It's about 125,000 gallons of water, and we had the ability to circulate upwards of 30,000 gallons per minute, which is a lot of water!

How many people do you have on your team?
On the *Black Panther* special effects crew we probably have around a 30-person crew. It's big, and it was big for all of us. It's been an exciting ordeal.

Have you done anything like this before?
This set was the largest water set that I've ever done. I've worked on a few water sets, but nothing of this scope or magnitude. One thing that was really exciting for me was that it was big. I was stepping into something that was huge.

What experience will this film deliver?
I think it's really going to be very exciting for the audience to be able to see *Black Panther* and find out a little bit more of his backstory and where he's going into the future. ■

02 Concept art for M'Kabu's entrance into Warrior Falls. Art by J. Straub

03 T'Challa faces a deadly challenge at Warrior Falls

04 Warrior Falls player M'Kabu, played by Winston Duke, with his tribal mask

05 Chadwick Boseman and Forest Whitaker filming in watery conditions

03

04

05

WEAPONS OF WAKANDA

A country rich in vibranium, Wakanda is protected from her enemies by a powerful arsenal of weapons that must never fall into the wrong hands...

01 Armed and dangerous: Erik Killmonger

02 Erik Killmonger dons his own Panther suit

03 Killmonger eyes up some Wakandan weponary at the British Museum

04 Knives out! Killmonger is armed and dangerous in production art by Rodney Fuentebella

05 Shuri takes aim with her Panther gauntlets

06 Shuri's gauntlets in detail.

KILLMONGER
KNIVES OUT
2016. 09

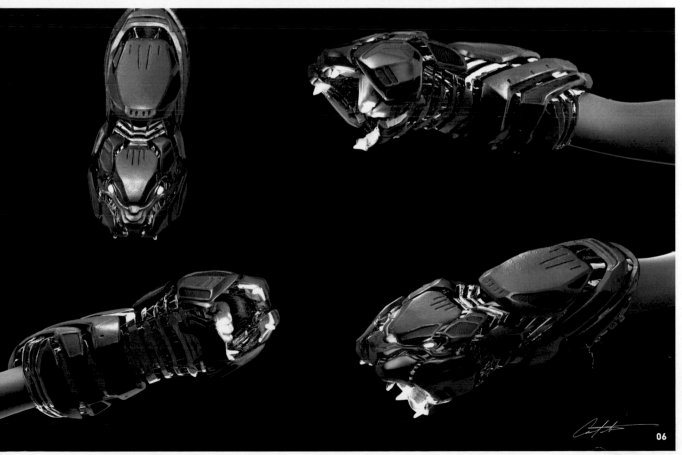

07 Okoye brandishes
her trusty spear

08 Dora Milaje ring
blades – a particular
favorite of Nakia

CONCEPT ART
Black Panther and Killmonger
engage in a deadly battle.
Art by Jackson Sze

MARVEL'S MASTERMIND

The President of Marvel Studios, Kevin Feige is the power behind the heroes. Currently overseeing the final part of the third phase of the Marvel Cinematic Universe, he took some time out from his busy schedule to discuss the much anticipated *Black Panther* movie.

Black Panther Movie Special: What kind of film can people expect from *Black Panther*?
Kevin Feige: One of the things that was so satisfying about *Captain America: Civil War* was being able to bring this story that we've loved for years to moviegoers. Seeing Iron Man and Captain America facing off against each other in a way that you wouldn't expect was something that we really loved and the reason we wanted to make the movie.

What was so exciting coming out of that production and seeing audiences' reactions, was the new characters that we introduced for the very first time. The character that really popped out of that

movie was the Black Panther, a character that's been around for over 50 years. He's been a staple of Marvel Comics for years and finally gets his big screen debut, and does so in a way where he steals the limelight from Iron Man and from Captain America.

People came out of that movie wanting to know more about that character and his world. That of course is exactly what we're doing in the *Black Panther* movie. Audiences can see Wakanda, see T'Challa's lineage, see Black Panther's other outfits, and meet the amazing, rich cast of characters that surround him.

The *Black Panther* movie deals with the repercussions of *Civil War* but then goes into the geopolitics of Wakanda. We have put together

a cast and a crew that is among the best that we've ever assembled, led by our director Ryan Coogler who is an unbelievable filmmaker. He's already made films that I believe will stand the test of time with *Fruitvale Station* and *Creed*.

Is there a specific sort of genre you're playing with for this film?
I think what people enjoy most about the Marvel Cinematic Universe is that the films are all very different. We try to make all of them stand apart. *Black Panther* really is unlike anything we've done before. We are introducing a country in the middle of Africa that has been secret for centuries, pulling back those layers and going in to see it and finding a technologically-advanced nation,

▶beyond anything currently on the planet. *How did that happen? How did they keep their secret? What happens if that secret gets out? How will T'Challa deal with the death of his father T'Chaka who was killed by trying to step out of the shadows and secrecy of Wakanda?* T'Challa is not that interested in embracing the larger world, but he's going to have to.

There are villains that we've met before that come into play, along with some new foes. What's exciting is that we deal with royal families, but unlike our other films it's not on alien planets, it's not on other sort of deep mythological roots like the *Thor* franchise; it's right here on Earth in this spectacular, amazing African nation.

Can you talk about the fantastic cast that has been assembled?
Ryan Coogler, who's directing the film, has assembled a spectacular cast. We have one of the most diverse casts ever assembled for a movie of this size. That's one of the things that's so exciting about it. We get to explore different cultures and different aspects of our world. That sense of diversity goes back to the original Marvel comic books. Marvel Comics has always represented society as it exists. The Black Panther character came about in the mid-1960s, during the time of the Civil Rights Movement, and debuted the same year as the Black Panther party.

And how daring it was for Stan Lee and Jack Kirby, and the team in the Marvel Bullpen, to say, "We're going to introduce a character named the Black Panther, an African character who is smarter than any of our other heroes, who is stronger than most of our other heroes, and who comes from a place which is more advanced and has more intelligence than anywhere else on Earth?" For Marvel Studios to be able to put that on the big screen is incredibly exciting for us. ■

03

04

05

01 (Previous spread) Marvel Studios' Kevin Feige on set with Ryan Coogler and Andy Serkis

02 (Previous spread) Chadwick Boseman as Black Panther

03 Action in the skies over Wakanda!

04 Michael B. Jordan as Erik Killmonger

05 Nakia and T'Challa enjoy a rare moment of peace

06 Sparks fly during a high octane car chase

07 Firestarter! Erik Killmonger watches as the palace burns

MR. MARVEL

STAN LEE ON BLACK PANTHER

Concept art of the Black
Panther leaping into
action from his Royal
Talon fighter jet.
Art by K. Le

"It was wonderful to be on the *Black Panther* set. When
you're working with professionals who do such a good
job and know what they're doing, you can see it working
out so beautifully. I'm so pleased because the Black
Panther's story is so important to me. This is such an
important movie – I'm just thrilled."

RYAN COOGLER

CALLING THE SHOTS IN WAKANDA

No stranger to the big screen, acclaimed director Ryan Coogler discusses what it was like bringing the breakout Super Hero of Marvel Studios' *Captain America: Civil War* into his own world...

01

How do the recent *Captain America* films relate to this movie?
They were a great platform to jump off of and go build this world. Captain America and Black Panther's worlds are closely related. There is the vibranium connection and the Super Soldier connection. But whereas Captain America tends to be a character that is easily defined, Black Panther exists in more of a gray area. In addition to being a soldier, he has a more important job as a politician. He's this guy who is a monarch, and he's constantly making difficult choices in the fog of politics and war.

How are you taking Chadwick's performance in *Civil War* and incorporating it now?
As a director you always want to work in concert with your actors. Chad's experience, crafting his character, is a big part of what the world around him looks like. The film is about Panther but equally about Wakanda. We'll see T'Challa's friends, people who he grew up with, people who he's responsible for, people he has to answer to when he's sitting on that throne. All of that is extremely important.
    And you have more understanding watching T'Challa do the things he did in *Civil War*, why he moved the way he moved.

How will you be exploring the drama of T'Challa's ascension to the throne?
It's the elephant in the room when you talk about the character and the events after *Civil War*. He's dealing with the loss of his father on a personal level, but also on a professional level. He just got the biggest promotion of his life, and it's a whole nation of people who are looking at him for what to do next.

Tell us about filming in Africa.
Going to Africa was extremely important because that's where the heart of the narrative takes place. The fact that Wakanda exists, in our film, on the continent ▶

*B*lack Panther Movie Special: When you took on the *Black Panther* movie, did you research the history of the character?
Ryan Coogler: Yes, we looked at everything. Black Panther has such a rich history. He's one of those characters that the writers do a good job of building on what the last custodian of the story did. Certain writers come on board and invent certain things about Wakanda, or build on the characters. You see those characters carry over and grow under the care of other writers.

How has it been working with Kevin Feige and the team at Marvel Studios?
They're very open with what they wanted from this project and the story they wanted to tell. Meeting Kevin Feige was really cool. Obviously I was familiar with all his work, being a comic book movie fan. He's somebody who really loves what he does, and has a really clear vision of what the Marvel universe means in pop culture, and what it can do. He can see the bigger picture, but at the same time is focused on character and story.

01 Ryan Coogler and Chadwick Boseman talk through a scene on location

02

of Africa, makes it much more complex. It's where the characters are from and that's how they identify. Getting to film there, and seeing the people and the incredible locations is amazing.

T'Challa also has to make sure the spotlight stays off Wakanda.
Absolutely. A big function of how Wakanda works is staying in the shadows. The less people know about Wakanda, the better from their perspective, which is becoming more and more challenging in this day and age. That was a big challenge for us; how is this place staying that way?

How does Michael B. Jordan fit into the film?
Chadwick's in this position where we have to find people around him who can support the narrative and support his performance, and bring the best out in him. We needed someone to challenge T'Challa. Mike fit that perfectly, and casting him was a no-brainer.
    Another big thing is being able to take actors who audiences are very familiar with and give them the opportunity – and the actor – to see him in a way that's different. I'm super excited about that with

03

Mike because I think, out of all of the characters, he's probably the biggest departure in terms of what we're used to seeing.

Why is Killmonger a threat?
I think Killmonger is a big threat to T'Challa because he truly understands Wakanda. They say if you know your enemy, then you're in pretty good shape. It makes you very formidable. That's really what society has come to – information. And that's what Killmonger has.

Will the audience be able to understand his point of view?
If we do our jobs right! I think as filmmakers and for this film to work, it has to be one that exists in the gray area, probably

more so than Super Hero-inspired films that have come before, because that's the world Panther lives in. And that's where all these characters live.

Let's talk about the leading ladies.
We have Lupita Nyong'o and Danai Gurira. Lupita's playing a character named Nakia who's got a very close personal relationship with T'Challa that dates back to when they were really young. Their relationship is complicated, circumstantially, and they are both involved with the Wakandan military. Their relationship is a big one in the film, and she's a really interesting character. She's one of the top fighters in Wakanda, but more so than that, she's very much T'Challa's equal.

02 Chadwick Boseman in his iconic Black Panther costume

03 Okoye and Nakia race through the streets of Busan in a thrilling car chase

04 T'Challa unmasked

"One thing that people might not know is that Panther's suit is not a Super Hero suit - it's a military uniform."

Danai plays Okoye, who's the head of the Dora Milaje and essentially second in command of the Wakanda military. She's a character who we're super excited about. I don't know if there's been anybody like either one of these characters, not just in the Marvel universe but in mainstream comic book movies in general. Their relationship is interesting as well.

What about costumes?
We've got Ruth Carter, who's an exceptional costume designer, working with Ryan Meinerding and the visual development team here at Marvel. Costumes are a big part of Wakanda; a lot of our decisions that we make come off what we're saying Wakandan culture is. We're looking at African culture, and one thing that's great about African culture is the clothing that people wear.

Wakanda is made up of different tribes, so we're getting into that through the clothes. The military ranking system has different clothing to it. One thing that a lot of people might not know is that Panther's suit is not a Super Hero suit. It's a military uniform that he wears and something that has a history – so we had a lot of fun there.

How has your experience been, working on this film?
Well, this is my third time making a movie. I'm still new to the process, and each time has been extremely different. Going from *Fruitvale* to *Creed* was like night and day. The budget was 30 times larger. You couldn't make a bigger jump. But at the same time, you're still finding yourself trying to deal with the same questions. You constantly ask yourself, what's this movie about? What's this character going through? What's the best way that we can tell this story in the fewest amount of script pages, so that we can shoot it in the days that we have budgeted?

Working with Marvel is so different from making *Creed*. We're doing concept art constantly. While we're working on the script we're doing everything at the same time. And because there's more to do you have way more people working on it. So you're getting an exponential increase on the ideas that are being presented to you and questions that you have to answer. But at the end of the day the hardest questions are the same ones.

What's the most exciting thing on a project like this?
I would be into this movie if I were an audience member – more than anything else I've seen before. Just the idea of bringing a story like this to fruition and characters like this to fruition – an African king who's also strong enough, fast enough, smart enough, to do some of the things that T'Challa's gonna do in this script, but at the same time deal with some of the human issues that I recognize as a regular guy – is so very exciting. What I most look forward to is sharing it with the audience and seeing how it impacts the little kids who are like I was. ∎

OTHER GREAT TIE-IN COMPANIONS FROM TITAN
ON SALE NOW!

Rogue One – The Official Collector's Edition
ISBN 9781785861574

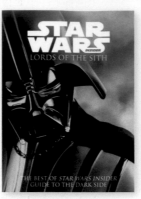

Rogue One – The Official Mission Debrief
ISBN 9781785861581

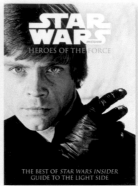

Star Wars: Lords of the Sith
ISBN 9781785851919

Star Wars: Heroes of the Force
ISBN 9781785851926

Star Wars: Icons of the Galaxy
ISBN 9781785851933

The Best of Star Wars Insider Volume 1
ISBN 9781785851162

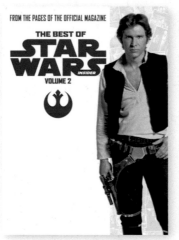

The Best of Star Wars Insider Volume 2
ISBN 9781785851179

The Best of Star Wars Insider Volume 3
ISBN 9781785851896

The Best of Star Wars Insider Volume 4
ISBN 9781785851902

Star Trek: The Movies
ISBN 9781785855924

Fifty Years of Star Trek
ISBN 9781785855931

Star Trek – A Next Generation Companion
ISBN 9781785855948

Star Trek Discovery Collector's Edition
ISBN 9781785861581

Thor Ragnarok Movie Special
ISBN 9781785866371

TITAN COMICS
For more information visit www.titan-comics.com